PLAN YOUR DEFENCE

FREDDIE NORTH

Foreword by BOBBY WOLFF

HOW TO PLAY BRIDGE

B T BATSFORD

First published 1998
© Freddie North 1998

ISBN 0 7134 8253 2

A CIP catalogue record for this book is available
from the British Library.

Typeset by Apsbridge Services Ltd, Nottingham.

Printed in Singapore
for the publishers,
B. T. Batsford Ltd, 583 Fulham Road,
London SW6 5BY

A BATSFORD BRIDGE BOOK
Series Editor: Tony Sowter
Commissioning Editor: Paul Lamford

contents

foreword

Bridge is a game enjoyed by many millions of players all over the world.

In these days of rising commercial pressures, increasing leisure and greater longevity, bridge has the potential to break down social and ethnic barriers and to keep the wheels of the brain turning in both the old and the young. Apart from that, bridge at whatever level is a very inexpensive game; all you need to play is a flat surface that the four players can sit round with a pack of cards and, of course, an understanding as to how to play the game.

It is for these reasons that I am particularly pleased to welcome the 'How to Play Bridge' series which has been specially designed to make the game easy to follow for beginners, no matter what their age. I believe that you will find the whole series well presented and particularly easy to read.

It is a curious fact, that over the years many of the great bridge authors have been British. Names like Victor Mollo, Hugh Kelsey, Skid Simon and Terence Reese still figure prominently in the USA lists of the greatest selling bridge books, so the fact that this series of books has been generated in Great Britain comes as no real surprise. I happen to know that all the authors have played bridge at International level so, in general terms, they should know what they are talking about. Furthermore, all of the books are based on the methods that are played all over the United States today. So, once you have learned, you should have little difficulty in getting a game whenever you want to.

I believe that after studying the 'How to Play Bridge' series you will not only be off to a good start, you will be totally enthralled by this great game.

Bobby Wolff
Dallas, Texas
March 1997

introduction

Bridge is divided into three main sections: Bidding, Play of the hand and Defense, and since you will be defending far more frequently than you will be playing the hand, it is perhaps the most vital area of all. By popular consent, however, it is also the most difficult, but then that very fact makes it the most rewarding.

The good news is that a little study of the basic elements of Defense can make an enormous difference to a bridge player's game, and the object of this book is to present the simple basics in a straight-forward and easy to understand way.

It is worth remembering that bridge is a game that gives tremendous pleasure to millions of people all over the world and a little know-how can only enhance that enjoyment. Have fun as you start to become a pillar of strength in Defense.

the opening lead

The defenders certainly have one major advantage over declarer and that is the choice of opening lead. The responsibility for this initiative lies with the defender on declarer's left. Sometimes the choice rests on little more than an educated guess, but much more often there are clues from the bidding, or an easy choice presents itself because of the solidity in one suit as opposed to the fragility in another (KQJ10 obviously being preferred to Q964).

The bidding is frequently revealing as the opposition exchange information about each other's hands in order to arrive at their optimum contract. Sometimes your partner will be a significant contributor, but in any case it always pays to listen carefully and build up a picture from the information supplied.

Consider the bidding before you lead.

If the auction has been economical with meaningful clues (e.g. 1♠ – 4♠ or 1NT – 3NT) then at least it pays to know the standard leads. While the choice of suit will not always be a matter of routine, the choice of card invariably falls into a standardised category. As we've already seen, the card combinations in some suits are so obviously more attractive than others that most defenders would select the more robust suit. For example, AKQ5 would surely be preferred to KJ84, and KQJ9 looks better than K1072. Most of the time this simple approach will be best, but there are different priorities when leading against suit contracts, no trumps or slams, and sometimes exceptional measures have to be taken. However, you may find the guidelines that follow a help.

leading against a suit contract

The major consideration is not to give away unnecessary tricks; thus the best leads are usually from the top of a high three-card honor sequence (AKQ, KQJ, QJ10), or partner's suit.

Leading partner's suit cannot be emphasised too strongly, especially when he has made an overcall. Indeed, sometimes he has overcalled with this very factor partially in mind, but whatever the circumstances at least the lead of partner's suit should warrant a high priority – and, if it does misfire, you are well-placed in the post mortem!

Leading partner's suit should have priority.

A singleton lead is always attractive when there is a realistic chance of obtaining a ruff, or ruffs, but can do more harm than good if the bidding and your own hand make it abundantly clear that your partner cannot possibly obtain the lead.

Suppose you are West, defending against 4♥ by South:

South	North
1♥	3♥
4♥	

and you hold either hand (a) or hand (b);

(a)   West
             ♠ 4
             ♥ A63
             ♦ KJ652
             ♣ KQ108

On this occasion East is marked with an almost worthless hand, so it would be very optimistic to hope that he could obtain the lead and give you a ruff. Lead the ♣K.

(b)   West
             ♠ 4
             ♥ K63
             ♦ J9752
             ♣ 10743

Now the singleton spade lead has a lot going for it. East is likely to have a card of entry, even if it is not the ♠A, and one ruff might be enough to defeat the game. Lead ♠4.

It is seldom a good idea to lead the ace when it is
unsupported by the king, (e.g. A863 or A9752)
but it is even worse to play a low card because on
a bad day you will either not make your ace at all,
or you will give declarer a trick to which he is not
entitled. Aces are meant to capture kings and that
role would not be fulfilled if West led the ace in the
following setting:

954

A863   QJ102

K7

The best advice for West with this holding is
to wait for East to play the suit through
declarer's strength.

Do not
underlead
aces against
suit contracts.

The lead of the ace from a suit
52) is

roken
ose
e
r.

have
strong
rom any other suit looks
a singleton trump – it may
holding. As West
st a contract
g hands:

(a)
    West
    ♠ Q1053
    ♥ 6
    ♦ K10654
    ♣ AQ9

South	North
1 ♥	1 ♠
3 ♥	4 ♥

The lead of the singleton heart is unlikely to damage the defence because the suit has been bid strongly. Furthermore, a lead from any of the other suits is unattractive. Lead ♥6.

(b)
    West
    ♠ 5
    ♥ AJ96
    ♦ Q972
    ♣ Q1053

South	North
1 ♠	2 ♦
2 ♠	3 ♠
4 ♠	

Now there is a real chance that a trump lead will kill a critical holding in partner's hand, say Qxx or J10xx. Lead the ♣3, the unbid suit.

A trump lead is often effective when you wish to cut down dummy's ruffs. You should play low from

(84, 873) and also from
elp to illustrate the value

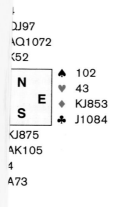

```
              ♠
              ♥ QJ97
              ♦ AQ1072
              ♣ K52
    ┌─────────┐   ♠ 102
    │    N    │   ♥ 43
    │  W   E  │   ♦ KJ853
    │    S    │   ♣ J1084
    └─────────┘
              ♠ KJ875
              ♥ AK105
              ♦ 4
              ♣ A73
```

      North
       2 ♦
       4 ♥

dding strongly
Of course, West
diamond suit,
e for discards, but he
will have to do
sing spades – and that
ng them in dummy.

followed up with a second
with one of his top spades,

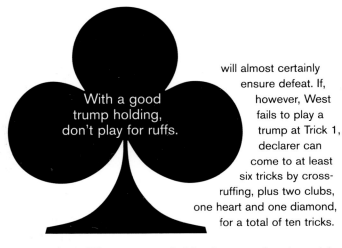

With a good trump holding, don't play for ruffs.

will almost certainly ensure defeat. If, however, West fails to play a trump at Trick 1, declarer can come to at least six tricks by cross-ruffing, plus two clubs, one heart and one diamond, for a total of ten tricks.

When your own holding in trumps is substantial, say K1095 or AJ96, it is usually profitable to lead from a long suit:

West
♠ KJ95
♥ 632
♦ KQ1052
♣ 6

South	North
1♠	2♥
2♠	3♠
4♠	

Lead the ♦K, not the ♣6. Plugging away with your long suit in the hope of weakening declarer's trumps is a better bet than playing for ruffs.

leading against no trumps

The priorities are now rather different as it is often necessary to build up winners in a long suit before declarer can establish enough tricks for his own contract. So often this develops into a race between the two sides. The defenders, with the advantage of the opening lead, may be prepared to give away a trick, or two, so long as they can achieve their main objective. With this end in mind the opening lead will frequently be a small card from a long suit. This suit may be headed by the ace, or even the ace and king – something that would be highly undesirable in a suit contract.

Choose your longest suit to lead against no trumps.

Study these examples:

West

(a)	♥	A96<u>4</u>3
(b)	♥	AK8<u>5</u>4
(c)	♥	A<u>Q</u>J96
(d)	♥	AQ7<u>6</u>3

Assuming West's long suit – in
has not been bid by North-Sout
underlined would be a normal lead against, say,
3NT by South.

Here is a full hand to illustrate the
advantage obtained by a defender after
making the traditional lead of fourth
highest of his longest and strongest
suit.

Dealer South.

```
                    ♠  KQ108
                    ♥  732
                    ♦  QJ6
                    ♣  A64
    ♠  632                        ♠  A975
    ♥  AK854        N             ♥  106
    ♦  8         W     E          ♦  9532
    ♣  10852        S             ♣  QJ9
                    ♠  J4
                    ♥  QJ9
                    ♦  AK1074
                    ♣  K73
```

South	North
1♦	1♠
1NT	2NT
3NT	

Lead ♥5

After the lead of the ♥5, the declarer can only run eight tricks (five diamonds, two clubs and one heart) and he will then have to play on spades. East will grab his ace and dutifully return his partner's suit (♥6). Returning partner's suit is often the best policy and I strongly recommend that you always make a mental note of the suit concerned. There is nothing worse than a defender waiting to cash sufficient winners to defeat the contract only to find that his partner doesn't know what to play because he has forgotten which suit partner led!

In the present case West, who will have retained all his hearts (he can throw two spades and two clubs on the run of the diamond suit), will now make four heart tricks to add to his partner's ♠A. So declarer has gone one down, but suppose West, untutored in the technique of opening leads, plays one top heart (just to have a look at dummy, partner) and then a small one, or cashes the AK – declarer is now home and dry because all communication with the East hand has been severed beyond recall. East will win the ♠A in due course but will then have nothing helpful to play and declarer, far from going down, will make no less

Remember which suit partner led.

than eleven tricks, or ten tricks if West cashes both the top heart honors.

When you are considering your opening lead don't forget partner's suit which always merits a high priority, especially if he has made an overcall. On the following hand everything hinges on the opening lead.

Dealer North.

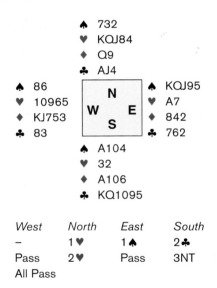

West	North	East	South
–	1♥	1♠	2♣
Pass	2♥	Pass	3NT
All Pass			

West's natural lead is the ♦5 – fourth highest of his longest and strongest suit – and this is no doubt what he would have chosen had it not been for his partner's overcall. But now he leads the ♠8 which enables East to establish his suit. Declarer has only seven top tricks and has to play on hearts for his additional winners, but East takes his ♥A and cashes his remaining spades for one down.

Note the difference if West fails to lead his partner's suit and plays a diamond instead (his longest suit). Declarer will now make at least ten tricks.

If one of the opponents bids your longest suit, and partner has not bid, it may be a good idea to try and hit partner's suit.

West
♠ J32
♥ 1097
♦ K10743
♣ 83

Suppose this is the bidding

West	North	East	South
–	–	–	1♦
Pass	1♠	Pass	1NT
Pass	3NT	All Pass	

In the normal way, West would lead the ♦4, but warned that South has a diamond suit he might well try and find his partner at home in hearts.

Let's look at the full deal:

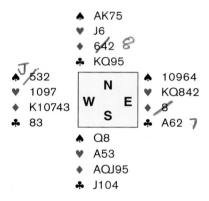

```
                    ♠ AK75
                    ♥ J6
                    ♦ 642
                    ♣ KQ95
        ♠ 532                    ♠ 10964
        ♥ 1097         N         ♥ KQ842
        ♦ K10743    W     E      ♦ 8
        ♣ 83           S         ♣ A62
                    ♠ Q8
                    ♥ A53
                    ♦ AQJ95
                    ♣ J104
```

Contract 3NT: Lead ♥ 10

After the lead of the ♥ 10 declarer has no chance, whereas a diamond lead would make it easy for him to collect nine tricks. The difference is that the heart lead enables East to establish his suit before his ♣A is knocked out. A diamond lead gives South the tempo to attack clubs while he still controls the heart suit.

leads against slams

Obviously great care is needed when leading against a small slam and while every case should be judged on its own merits there are some useful general guidelines.

Against a small slam in a suit it is often best to attack, i.e. lead away from an honor in an attempt to set up a trick before declarer can knock out a vital control which then enables him to discard losers. Of course, if partner is marked with a worthless hand then it is best to find a safe lead.

Attack when your opponents bid a small slam in a suit.

The following examples illustrate these points:

West
- ♠ 52
- ♥ 10973
- ♦ 643
- ♣ K862

West finds himself on lead against Six Spades after South has opened 1 ♠ and North has shown a strong hand with a diamond suit and spade support.

Following general principles, West should lead the ♣ 2, and while this opening is not guaranteed to defeat the slam it would do so in this not so unlikely setting:

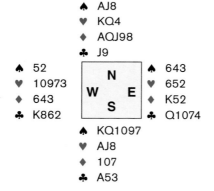

```
              ♠  AJ8
              ♥  KQ4
              ♦  AQJ98
              ♣  J9
  ♠ 52                      ♠ 643
  ♥ 10973     N             ♥ 652
  ♦ 643     W   E           ♦ K52
  ♣ K862      S             ♣ Q1074
              ♠  KQ1097
              ♥  AJ8
              ♦  107
              ♣  A53
```

You can see that any lead other than a club gives declarer time to establish his diamond suit for two club discards. Of course, South might have had ♣ AQ5 but if that is the case no harm is done because there is only one trick for the defense no matter what is led.

West
- ♠ 1094
- ♥ K4
- ♦ K962
- ♣ J1076

This time West is on lead against Six Hearts, North having shown a strong hand with a club suit and heart support. With West holding so many key cards himself, it is unlikely that East can contribute much to the defense, so West should lead the ♠10. If the full hand turns out to be as follows, West may be rewarded with two tricks – one heart and one diamond.

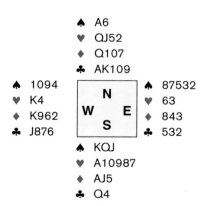

                    ♠ A6
                    ♥ QJ52
                    ♦ Q107
                    ♣ AK109
    ♠ 1094   ♠ 87532
    ♥ K4   N   ♥ 63
    ♦ K962   W   E   ♦ 843
    ♣ J876   S   ♣ 532
                    ♠ KQJ
                    ♥ A10987
                    ♦ AJ5
                    ♣ Q4

With the sight of all four hands the declarer could make his slam by finessing the ♣10, but in practice he is likely to take a losing trump finesse and then when the ♣J doesn't come down take a losing diamond finesse.

Against small slams in No Trumps it is usually correct to make a safe lead. If the opponents have no long suits to run, they will have to locate a missing honor or two.

Suppose the bidding has gone:

South	North
2NT	4NT
6NT	

and West holds:

♠ Q852
♥ 73
♦ 109
♣ K10865

Against Three No Trumps, West would no doubt lead the ♣6 if that suit had not been bid by his opponents. Against 6NT, however, he must try and find a safe lead. That rules out the black suits leaving West to choose between the ♥7 and ♦10. Since the diamond holding is a little more substantial than the hearts he starts with the ♦10.

Against 6NT, try and find a safe lead.

This is the full hand:

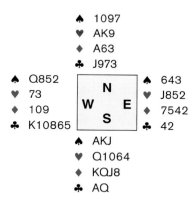

```
                ♠ 1097
                ♥ AK9
                ♦ A63
                ♣ J973
   ♠ Q852                        ♠ 643
   ♥ 73          ┌─────────┐     ♥ J852
   ♦ 109         │    N    │     ♦ 7542
   ♣ K10865      │ W     E │     ♣ 42
                 │    S    │
                 └─────────┘
                ♠ AKJ
                ♥ Q1064
                ♦ KQJ8
                ♣ AQ
```

Contract 6NT by South. Lead ♦ 10.

Fortunately for the defenders the lead has given nothing away and if declarer thinks his best chance is to take both the black suit finesses the slam will fail.

Against grand slams, whether in a suit or in No Trumps, always make a safe lead. After all, you don't need to establish a trick – you just need to avoid giving one away.

second hand plays low

The heading of this chapter does not constitute a rule, or a command, it simply suggests a commonsense principle, emanating from the days of Whist, which will be correct most of the time in normal circumstances.

Having said that, there are many exceptions, some quite obvious, some more obscure, but this book is not designed to deal with the esoteric, exotic or obscure. It just covers the everyday defensive situations which occur with great frequency and thus form a valuable base for the aspiring learner.

As a generalisation, the advantage of second player playing low is that it may give the third player quite a problem when, as so often happens, he has an unenviable choice to make. Furthermore, the second player has a partner who plays last of all. If the second player has not committed himself, it leaves the third player with all the guesswork while the fourth player waits to take advantage of any favourable situation that may develop.

The following examples should help to demonstrate some of the advantages of the second player playing low.

(a)   Dummy
                       864
        Q10752   A63
                       KJ

The four is led from dummy towards the concealed hand of declarer. If East rushes up with the ace declarer has no guess and loses just one trick. If, however, East follows the general advice of "second player plays low", and does so at normal tempo so as not to give his hand away, declarer is faced with a losing option. If he decides to insert the jack he will lose two tricks.

(b)   Dummy
                       752
        J93   A1064
                       KQ8

The two is led from dummy towards the closed hand. If East now gets itchy fingers and goes up

with the ace, declarer's
problems are over. If,
however, East ducks,
declarer will have to
utilise a further
entry to dummy in
order to make his
second trick in the suit.
Sometimes there is no
further entry, or if there is, it
may be needed for something
else, so there is much to be said
for playing low on the first round.

Do not take your aces too quickly.

Alter the scene a little and we get this:

(c)   Dummy
                       KQ104
        A72   J85
                       963

A small card is played towards dummy and the
king is allowed to win. Declarer gets back to hand
and again plays low towards dummy. If West
ducks again declarer is faced with a choice.
Should he go up with the queen or insert the ten?
After all, the full layout might be like this:

                       Dummy
                       KQ104
        J72   A85
                       963

On this occasion it is East who has not committed himself on the first round, but declarer has to guess which defender is holding back.

(d)   Dummy
                  AJ9
      KQ6   10873
                  542

Declarer leads the two towards dummy. If West plays low declarer will probably insert the nine – the best percentage shot – and lose two tricks in the suit. If West plays an honor on the first round, declarer is likely to play him for both king and queen and lose just one trick.

(e)   Dummy
                  J74
      K82   Q95
                  A1063

Declarer plays the three towards dummy. If West goes up with the king, declarer will be able to make three tricks in the suit by taking a simple finesse through East when he next gets to dummy. If West plays low on the first round, declarer will be restricted to just two tricks.

It is rather more difficult for West when he holds Kx or Qx in a similar setting to (e), but even then it is usually correct to play low.

(f)   Dummy
                   J74
        K6   Q98
                   A10532

Declarer plays a low card towards dummy and if
West's nerves are strong enough he may save
a trick for his side by ducking at normal
tempo. East wins this trick with his queen
and subsequently West may make his
king as declarer goes to dummy and
finesses East for this card. If West
goes up with the king on the first
round there will be no more losers
when declarer enters dummy and
finesses East for the queen.

Duck in normal tempo.

(g)   Dummy
                   QJ953
        K1086   A
                   742

Declarer plays a low card towards
dummy. If West goes up with the king it
will fall under his partner's ace for a
disastrous result.

Having seen the plus side of "second player plays
low" it is important not to lose sight of the logical
approach. Regardless of slogans, popular doctrine
and folklore, it is essential that commonsense
always prevails. So if, for example, you were

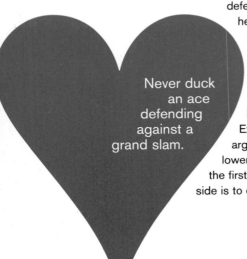

Never duck
an ace
defending
against a
grand slam.

defending against 7NT and held an ace as second player it would be absurd to play low. There might not be a second chance so that playing low would be a very costly error. Exactly the same argument applies to all lower level contracts where the first duty of the defending side is to defeat the contract.

third hand plays high

Perhaps this advice should be qualified by: "But don't forget to take note of the cards in dummy before playing one of yours."

For example, if this is the layout:

Dummy

```
              Q73
   10842              KJ5
              A96
```

West plays the two, dummy plays the three and East? Yes, obviously the jack, not the king. But you won't know that unless you have looked at dummy's holding. Of course, if dummy has just three small cards, then the king would be the card to play.

Look at dummy <u>before</u> playing your card.

The whole idea of contributing a high card as third player is based on the precept that it may result

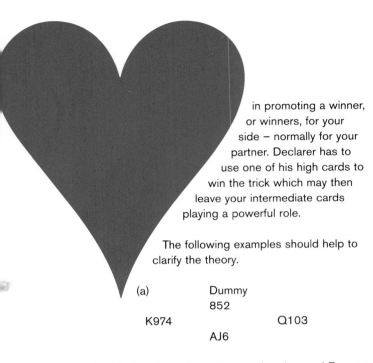

in promoting a winner, or winners, for your side – normally for your partner. Declarer has to use one of his high cards to win the trick which may then leave your intermediate cards playing a powerful role.

The following examples should help to clarify the theory.

(a)   Dummy
             852
K974   Q103
             AJ6

West leads the four, dummy plays low and East, as third player, must follow with the queen. Declarer wins with the ace, but now his J6 will subsequently be trapped under West's K9. Note the difference if East contributes a feeble ten to this first trick. A grateful declarer will win with the jack and still have his ace in reserve.

(b)   Dummy
             962
K1043   AJ5
             Q87

West leads the three and whatever dummy plays it is essential that East plays the ace (third player plays high) so that the defense make all three tricks in the suit.

If East makes the mistake of playing the jack, declarer will win an undeserved trick with the queen.

(c)   Dummy
                             74
        A10852   KJ6
                             Q93

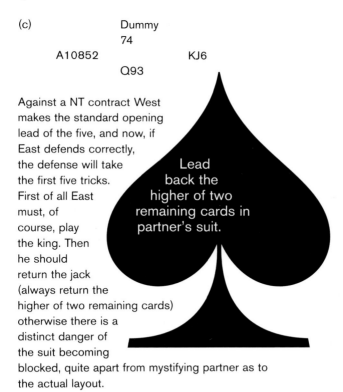

Against a NT contract West makes the standard opening lead of the five, and now, if East defends correctly, the defense will take the first five tricks. First of all East must, of course, play the king. Then he should return the jack (always return the higher of two remaining cards) otherwise there is a distinct danger of the suit becoming

Lead back the higher of two remaining cards in partner's suit.

blocked, quite apart from mystifying partner as to the actual layout.

(d)   Dummy
                          974
        K863   QJ2
                          A105

West leads the three and now it is imperative that
East plays the right card. High, of course, but he
must play the jack, not the queen. The reason for
this is to help partner. If the jack loses to the ace
West will know that his partner is virtually certain
to hold the queen.

The simple rule for East is to follow with the lower
card of equals – or the lowest of equals if he holds
three (or more) in a row (i.e. the ten from QJ10)

(e)   Dummy
                          965
        10842   KQ3
                          AJ7

The two is led and East correctly
follows with the queen and South wins
with the ace. At this point West knows
that South holds the jack (East would not
play the queen if he held the jack as well) but
cannot be certain of the position of the king.
However, he does know that East may hold the
king.

third hand plays intermediate

At the beginning of the section on "Third hand plays high" you were advised to note the cards in dummy before playing one of your own. This theme is now developed more fully because, despite all that has been said about third hand playing high, there are many occasions when an intermediate card is correct. This card is usually the second highest. Of course, if there are only small cards in dummy then third hand invariably plays high, but, if there is an honor card on the table, third player usually gains by playing an intermediate card if it is available.

In the examples which follow East should assume that his partner has led from a holding headed by an honor. The bidding, which is always the key to these situations, precludes the likelihood of it being a singleton.

(a)   Dummy
                       Q64
        K862   AJ9
                       1053

West leads the two, dummy plays small and
East....? East should play the jack, enabling the
defense to avoid the loss of a single trick. Note
what happens if East contributes the ace instead
of the jack. Now dummy's queen must make a trick
on the third round of the suit. Of course, the full
layout might be like this:

                       Dummy
                       Q64
        10862   AJ9
                       K53

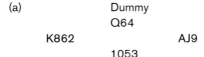

In third seat,
hold back your
honor to cover
dummy's if
you can.

Now East's jack loses to
the king, but dummy's
Q6 are trapped
under East's A9.
So in this case by
playing the jack
East restricts his
side's losses to just
one trick. By playing
the ace he would
concede two tricks.

(b)
          Dummy
          AJ9
    Q765   K104
          832

West leads the five, dummy plays the nine and East …? East should play the ten. If West has led from the queen, the ten will win the trick and the defense will make a second trick later on. If, however, East plays the king on the first round declarer will lose only one trick when later he finesses West for the queen.

(c)
          Dummy
          Q74
    J852   K109
          A63

West leads the two, dummy plays the four and East….? East should play the nine (the ten would deny the nine). Against a suit contract, West would not lead a low card from ace to four (Axxx) so it is almost certain that he holds the jack. Even against a no trump contract East should play the nine on dummy's four because this will not cost a trick. Subsequently the defense will be able to cash three tricks in the suit.

If declarer wins the first trick with the ace, East will have to wait for his partner to regain the lead so that he can play through dummy's Q7 which will then be captured by East's K10.

(d)

	Dummy	
	Q62	
10753		KJ8
	A93	

West leads the three and when dummy plays low it is fairly obvious for East to play the jack. Maybe declarer wins this trick with the ace which leaves East's king good: but the interesting point now is that the suit is 'frozen'. That is to say neither side can play it again without giving away a trick. From a defensive point of view East/West will do well if they try and make declarer play this suit next – then they will score two tricks. Say declarer plays the nine, West will cover with the ten and now dummy's Q6 will fall victim to East's K8, and if declarer chooses the three, West will play low and dummy's queen will lose to the king. West's ten will take the third round.

(e)

	Dummy	
	J42	
K1096		Q83
	A75	

West leads the ten, dummy plays the two and East…? East should play the three. Only if the jack is played from dummy (or dummy started with three small cards) would it be correct to play the queen. The reason that this combination of cards is different from the others is because West has started with an honor card. A similar situation arises when the cards fall like this:

Play
the lower
of equals in
third seat.

```
              Dummy
              Q74
J1095                    K63
              A82
```

West leads the jack and East only contributes the king if the queen is played from dummy.

(f)
```
              Dummy
              Q92
K863                     AJ10
              754
```

West leads the three, dummy plays the nine and East …? East should play the ten (the lower of equals). If West has led from the king the defense will take all the tricks in the suit. In the unlikely event of South having the king, he will win this trick but then East's AJ over dummy's Q2 will ensure two tricks for the defense when West plays this suit again.

(g)

```
            Dummy
            972
Q653                    J108
            AK4
```

West leads the three, dummy plays low and East …? As East can see the nine in dummy he should play the eight. When South wins with the ace or king West will know that his partner holds the J10 and therefore will be able to continue the suit safely.

(h)

```
            Dummy
            Q93
AJ752                   K104
            86
```

In no trumps, West leads the five, dummy plays the nine and East …? East should play the ten. If West's suit is headed by the AJ the defense will take all the tricks. If, however, South has the jack one trick will have to be lost anyway.

(i)   Dummy
                       Q8
       A97532   K106
                       J4

Against a no trump contract West leads the five,
dummy plays the eight and East …? Now East
should play the king in case the cards are as
shown in the diagram. If South held Ax or Axx, he
would surely put up dummy's queen.

the rule of eleven

When your partner leads the fourth highest card of a suit it is sometimes useful to know how many cards higher than the one led are held by declarer.

This information can be readily obtained by deducting the pips on the card led from eleven. The answer indicates how many higher cards are held by dummy, you and declarer. Here is a simple example.

Dummy
♥ J87

♥ K93

West leads ♥ 5. Contract 3 ♦

On West's lead of the ♥ 5 dummy plays the seven. Which card should East play?

Without knowledge of the Rule of Eleven East could hardly be blamed for, following general principles of "Third player plays high", playing the King, but it would cost a trick if this is the position:

Dummy
♥ J87
♥ Q1065   ♥ K93
♥ A42

You can see now that the nine is the right card to play as that will force the ace and leave the defense with all the winners.

Deducting West's lead – the five – from eleven leaves six better cards between the other three hands. Three are in dummy and East has two, so that leaves declarer with just one. As West is most unlikely to underlead an ace when opening the attack it is fair to presume that South's one card better that the five is the ace.

Use the Rule of Eleven to tell you how many cards declarer has higher than the card led.

If East doesn't apply his new-found technique to the problem and plays the king, declarer will win with the ace and later make a second trick as he leads towards dummy's jack.

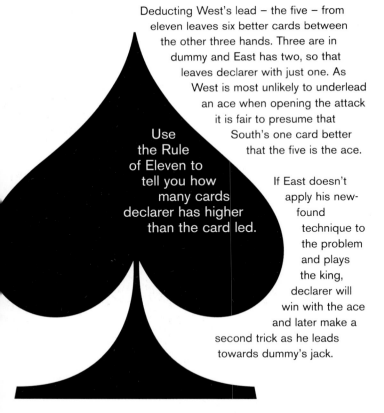

See what you make of East's problem on the next
hand.

North	South
1♠	2♥
3♥	4♥

Dummy
♠ AK542
♥ 1098
♦ AJ8
♣ Q6

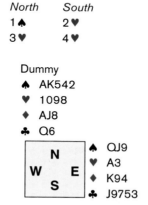

♠ QJ9
♥ A3
♦ K94
♣ J9753

West leads ♦6.

On the ♦6 dummy plays the eight. Now how
should East defend?

This is the full hand:

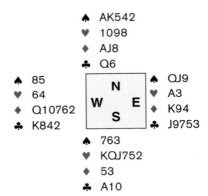

```
              ♠ AK542
              ♥ 1098
              ♦ AJ8
              ♣ Q6
  ♠ 85                      ♠ QJ9
  ♥ 64          N           ♥ A3
  ♦ Q10762  W     E         ♦ K94
  ♣ K842        S           ♣ J9753
              ♠ 763
              ♥ KQJ752
              ♦ 53
              ♣ A10
```

Looking at all four hands it seems that there is a loser in each suit, but declarer decides to put East under pressure immediately. If East follows with the king on dummy's eight, declarer will subsequently be able to finesse West for the queen and discard his losing club on dummy's ♦ A. He will then lose just one diamond, one heart and one spade.

If, however, East applies the Rule of Eleven he will know that South has no card higher than the six and his nine will take the trick.

The Rule of Eleven should help to make life easy for East on the following hand:

South	North
1NT	3NT

Dummy
- ♠ 109
- ♥ J74
- ♦ J862
- ♣ AKQ4

♠ Q76
♥ 1085
♦ A94
♣ 10983

West leads ♠5.

East covers dummy's nine of spades with the queen and South wins with the king. Declarer now enters dummy with the ♣A and plays the ♦J. Which card should East play and why?

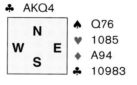

Work out what your partner has led from.

This is the full hand:

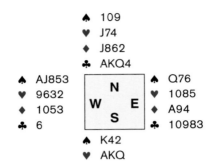

♠ 109
♥ J74
♦ J862
♣ AKQ4

♠ AJ853
♥ 9632
♦ 1053
♣ 6

N
W E
S

♠ Q76
♥ 1085
♦ A94
♣ 10983

♠ K42
♥ AKQ
♦ KQ7
♣ J752

East should go in smartly with the
♦ A and play the ♠ 7. The Rule of
Eleven has indicated quite
clearly that declarer has no
more high cards in spades
and West is waiting to
cash his winners.

**Don't
duck a
side suit
ace when
partner's suit
is running.**

Declarer's play of
the ♦ J from dummy
was an attempt to steal
a trick which would then
enable him to run for home.

Finally, the Rule of Eleven was the saving grace on the following hand:

North	South
North	*South*
1 ♥	1NT
3NT	

Dummy
♠ K52
♥ AKQJ84
♦ A10
♣ J4

```
        N
    W       E
        S
```

♠ AJ93
♥ 96
♦ 742
♣ AK52

West leads ♠ 7.

On West's ♠ 7 dummy plays the two.
Which card should East play?

The full hand

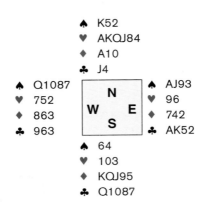

```
              ♠ K52
              ♥ AKQJ84
              ♦ A10
              ♣ J4
  ♠ Q1087                    ♠ AJ93
  ♥ 752          N           ♥ 96
  ♦ 863      W       E       ♦ 742
  ♣ 963          S           ♣ AK52
              ♠ 64
              ♥ 103
              ♦ KQJ95
              ♣ Q1087
```

The only way to defeat this contract is for East to appreciate that if his partner's lead is the fourth highest then declarer can't have a card higher than the seven (7 from 11 =4 and East can see 3 cards better in his own hand and 1 in dummy). So East must play the 3. When West continues the suit nothing can stop the defense taking four spades and two clubs.

Just note the difference if East plays any card other that the three. He is now on lead and there is no longer any way to defeat the contract.

covering honors and when not to

It would make life much easier if there was a hard and fast rule that made it quite clear when an honor should be covered – and when it shouldn't. However, there are some useful guide lines which will point you in the right direction most of the time.

Always cover an honor with an honor if there is any chance of your side winning a trick, or extra trick as a result. Never cover if the bidding, or probable distribution of the cards, suggests that there is nothing to be gained by covering.

Don't cover when there is nothing to be gained.

The following examples, which relate to a side suit – not the trump suit which is dealt with separately – will help to clarify the situation.

(a)   Dummy
                   Q4
862   K109
                   AJ753

When the queen is played from dummy East must cover with the king otherwise declarer will make all the tricks in this suit. Even if East is missing the ten (say K92) he should cover in the hope that he can promote a trick for his partner (say 1086)

(b)   Dummy
                   J5
9643   Q82
                   AK107

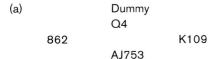

The jack is led from dummy and this time East cannot see any potential gain for his hand by covering, but there is always the chance that partner may be the beneficiary – as indeed is the case here. When East covers the jack with the queen, West's nine will subsequently be promoted to winning rank. If East fails to cover, South will finesse the ten on the next round and make all four tricks in the suit.

(c)   Dummy
                       QJ8
        1064   K52
                       A973

The queen is led from dummy. Should East
cover? The simple advice here is not to
cover the first honor, but to cover the
second. Let's just follow the reason
for this proposal. Suppose the
play goes Q,K,A,4. Now, on the
way back to dummy, declarer
can pick up West's ten by
finessing dummy's eight. So
he doesn't lose a trick at all. If,
however, East refrains from
covering the queen and waits to
cover the jack, West's ten will win a trick
on the third round.

With two touching honors in dummy, cover the second.

(d)   Dummy
                       QJ108
        7   K632
                       A954

The queen is led form dummy. Should East cover?

With such a solid holding in dummy there is
nothing to be gained by covering. In this particular
case it may not matter much what East does but it
would be helpful to South if East covered when
this was the distribution:

```
                Dummy
                QJ108
        74                      K632
                A95


(e)             Dummy
                J105
        K983                    Q74
                A62
```

The jack is led from dummy. Should East cover? The general guide of covering the second honor rewards the defenders in this case. The jack is run to West's king and only when the ten is played should East part with his queen. This defense will hold South to just one trick.

Note the difference when East covers the jack on the first round. South wins with the ace and then leads towards dummy to make his second trick.

There are some exceptions to covering the second honor or the second of equals and these usually arise when a defender has two honors, or perhaps when he has a doubleton.

(f)   Dummy
                       1094
        A875   KJ2
                       Q63

The ten is led from dummy. Which card should East play? East should cover with the jack enabling the defense to take all the tricks in the suit.

(g)   Dummy
                       J108
        K542   Q9
                       A763

The jack is led from dummy. Should East cover? East's best chance is to cover the jack with the queen. If South wins and then decides to finesse the eight on the next round the defense will come to two tricks instead of one. There will be no chance of a second trick if the first round goes J,9,3,K.

(h)   Dummy
                       AJ1095
        K7642   8
                       Q3

Declarer leads the queen. Should West cover? West should refuse to cover. As long as he does not commit the king on the first two rounds this card may eventually take a trick.

There is one situation where, despite the general advice to cover the second honor, it is correct to play your king immediately even though dummy holds QJx. This usually happens in no trumps where your priorities may be a little different in that a) you wish to assist partner to establish his suit and b) you plan to use your winners and preserve his so that he has an entry to enjoy his long suit when it becomes good.

The following hand illustrates this technique.

North	South
1♠	1NT
2NT	3NT

Lead ♥Q

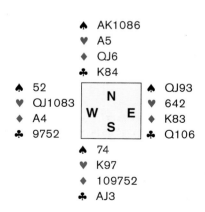

♠ AK1086
♥ A5
♦ QJ6
♣ K84

♠ 52
♥ QJ1083
♦ A4
♣ 9752

N
W E
S

♠ QJ93
♥ 642
♦ K83
♣ Q106

♠ 74
♥ K97
♦ 109752
♣ AJ3

Against South's contract of 3NT West leads the ♥Q which is allowed to win. The heart continuation goes to dummy's ace and declarer now plays the ♦Q which is the moment of truth for East.

As this is a No Trump contract, East should realise that anything he can do to help his partner establish his suit may be vital. Also, if West has the ♦A it will be equally important to let him retain it while East uses his king to win and clear the hearts.

If it turns out that South has the ♦A then nothing will be lost by East playing his king immediately. In fact, when East wins Trick 3 with the ♦K and plays a third heart, there is no way declarer can muster nine tricks before the defense make five.

Note the difference though when East ducks the ♦Q. West wins with the ace and can play a third heart to establish his suit, but this will be an abortive exercise as he has no card of re-entry. Declarer will simply knock-out the ♦K and make his contract in top tricks.

should a trump honor be covered

As the opposition have chosen their own trump suit there will be less opportunity to profit from covering their honors, especially when there has been meaningful support (1♠–4♠ or 1♥–3♥).

All too often declarer will be the only one to profit by covering so the general rule is 'Don't cover unless it is fairly obvious that your side may benefit'.

In the examples that follow we are, of course, considering just the trump suit.

(a)
```
              Dummy
              J1087
    6                      Q42
              AK1053
```

Declarer cashes the ace and then enters dummy to play the jack. There is absolutely no point in East covering so he must play low, at normal tempo. It is quite probable that declarer intends playing his king anyway, but it costs nothing to try and get some help from East before finally committing himself.

(b)   Dummy
                            J652
        A   K3
                            Q109874

Declarer may play the jack from dummy, tempting a
cover, but East should have nothing to do with it.
When he follows with the three a catastrophe is
averted, but full marks to declarer for trying!

Sometimes there is another reason for not
covering. Suppose the cards fall like this:

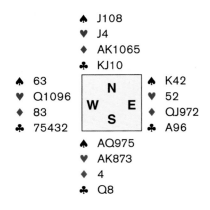

♠ J108
♥ J4
♦ AK1065
♣ KJ10

♠ 63
♥ Q1096
♦ 83
♣ 75432

♠ K42
♥ 52
♦ QJ972
♣ A96

♠ AQ975
♥ AK873
♦ 4
♣ Q8

Contract: 6♠ by South. Lead ♠3.

Having shown a two-suited hand in the majors,
South arrives in the slightly ambitious contract of
6♠.

Having a respectable holding in hearts (declarer's second suit), West decides to lead a trump. Dummy plays the jack and East …?

East must play a small card. Even if declarer continues with the ♠10 East should refuse to cover. It is inconceivable that by covering East can promote a trick for his side, but far more important is to cater for the possibility of overruffing dummy. Declarer will want to do something with his losing hearts and that, likely enough, means trumping in dummy.

If East does part with his ♠K on the first or second round, declarer will make his contract by ruffing a heart in dummy. Five spades, two hearts, one heart ruff, two diamonds and two clubs totals 12 tricks.

Try not to crash partner's singleton honor.

When the trump suit has not been supported and there is a meagre offering in dummy, it may be advantageous to cover an honor since there is some chance of partner having values that can be promoted.

In the next two examples South has just made a simple rebid of his suit.

(c)   Dummy
                       J3
        9654   Q2
                       AK1087

Dummy plays the jack and East promotes a trick for his side by covering with the queen.

(d)   Dummy
                       J3
        84   Q105
                       AK9762

When the jack is played from dummy East's best shot is to cover. His ten may get picked up later on but at least he's in with a chance.

(e)   Dummy
                       ♥ 105
        ♥ 2   ♥ Q73
                       ♥ AKJ9864

This time South jumped to 4 ♥ over his partner's opening bid of 1 ♦, so he is likely to have a seven card suit.

When the ♥ 10 is played East should not cover. There can't be anything to promote so one must avoid helping declarer. He is probably just fishing.

don't give a ruff and sluff

One of the plays to avoid – at least most of the time – is the Ruff and Sluff (or Ruff and Discard). That is to say leading a suit in which dummy and declarer are void while both still hold trumps.

West to lead – Hearts are trumps.

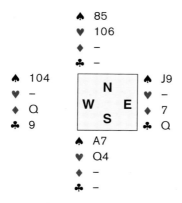

Declarer can make two trumps and the ♠A giving him three winners from the last four tricks. But suppose West leads a club or a diamond, now declarer will make all the tricks as he ruffs in one hand (say ♥6 from dummy) and discards from the other (♠7). Had West led a spade the Ruff and Sluff would have been avoided and declarer would have made only three tricks.

This is the sort of hand where an inexperienced defender might go wrong.

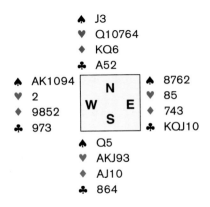

	♠	J3
	♥	Q10764
	♦	KQ6
	♣	A52

♠	AK1094
♥	2
♦	9852
♣	973

♠	8762
♥	85
♦	743
♣	KQJ10

	♠	Q5
	♥	AKJ93
	♦	AJ10
	♣	864

Contract 4♥ by South.

South	North
1♥	4♥

Declarer is up against it here as apparently he has four losers – two spades and two clubs. But suppose West cashes the ♠AK and then, wrongly, continues with a third spade. Now declarer will get rid of a club loser from one hand while he ruffs in the other. Contract made thanks to the Ruff and Sluff.

discarding

When you are unable to follow suit, and do not wish to ruff or you are defending a no trump contract, you have to make a discard and this is without doubt one of the most difficult areas of defensive play. It would be comforting if I could say, 'Throw away what you don't want and retain anything that may be useful', but that would only touch the periphery of the problem, although, to be fair, that is often what it comes down to.

You may find the following guidelines helpful.

1. Try to keep a long suit covered. For example, if you see a four or five-card suit in dummy and you hold four or five cards in the same suit, then you should endeavour to retain control of it.

                    Dummy
                    ♦ AKQ4
    ♦ J72   ♦ 10965
                    Declarer
                    ♦ 83

In this example if East parts with just one diamond all dummy's cards will be good.

Sometimes you can infer the length of a suit held by declarer simply by listening to the bidding.

South	North
1♥	1♠
2♣	3♥
4♥	

Suppose this has been the North-South bidding sequence and East holds ♣J952.

It is more than likely that South holds four clubs so East should try not to part with one unless there are greater priorities elsewhere.

Try to keep a long suit covered.

2. Maintaining a link with partner's hand, especially when he has winners that he is waiting to cash, is an essential ingredient of good defense.

Let's watch this action from both sides of the table.

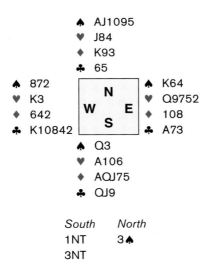

```
              ♠ AJ1095
              ♥ J84
              ♦ K93
              ♣ 65
    ♠ 872                    ♠ K64
    ♥ K3          N          ♥ Q9752
    ♦ 642     W     E        ♦ 108
    ♣ K10842     S           ♣ A73
              ♠ Q3
              ♥ A106
              ♦ AQJ75
              ♣ QJ9
```

South   North
1NT   3♠
3NT

Contract: 3NT by South. Lead ♣4.

East wins the first trick with the ♣A and correctly returns the ♣7. Reading the position for what it is, West follows with the two to retain a link with his partner's hand. You'll notice that West, having conceded one trick, now has three club winners to cash.

Perhaps declarer runs five diamonds
before tackling spades in which
case East will have to find
three discards. Well, the one
card he should not throw away
is the ♣3 – the link to partner's
hand. In fact, he can easily spare
one spade and two hearts. West has
no problem and discards two spades.
Eventually East will get in with the ♠K
and then a club return will defeat the
contract.

3. It can be a mistake to discard worthless
cards if that means exposing the position
to declarer in a critical suit.

Study the following:

```
                    ♠  1064
                    ♥  K863
                    ♦  KJ94
                    ♣  A10
    ♠  KQJ9        ┌──────────┐      ♠  872
    ♥  42          │    N     │      ♥  A5
    ♦  763         │ W     E  │      ♦  Q82
    ♣  J852        │    S     │      ♣  Q9763
                   └──────────┘
                    ♠  A53
                    ♥  QJ1097
                    ♦  A105
                    ♣  K4
```

South	North
–	Pass
1♥	3♥
4♥	

Contract: 4♥ by South. Lead ♠K.

With all four hands on view it is obvious that
declarer will lose two spades and the ace
of hearts, so success is going to
depend on finding the ♦ Q. Let's
see how the defenders can do
their best to camouflage the
position.

Small cards in a key suit can be valuable.

Declarer wins the ♠A and
plays a trump to East's ace.
East returns his partner's suit
enabling West to cash two spade
tricks and exit safely with a trump.

Maybe declarer cashes the ♣AK
and then starts to run the
remainder of his trumps, hoping for some help from
the discards. It may seem to West that his three
small diamonds are expendable, and so they are in
the sense that they will neither take a trick nor help
to do so, but there are more important issues at
stake. The first card that West can throw is the
thirteenth spade. it is of no use to him. Then there is
the club suit. If declarer had any club losers he
could have ruffed them in dummy so it is fair to

presume – regardless of any help from East's discards – that there are no losers in this suit. So the position is clear. West's three discards should be one spade and two clubs. East, of course, has to keep the ♦ Q so he discards three clubs.

With no help from the defense declarer will simply have to guess. But just imagine that West had thrown two, or even three, little diamonds. Now, surely, declarer would draw the right inference and play East for the queen.

4. Sometimes a defender finds himself in an impossible position of being unable to afford a discard of any kind. However, this situation is often not quite so desperate as it might appear.

Here is a fairly common scenario:

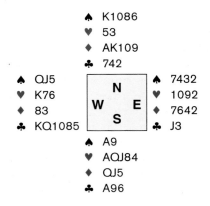

```
                 ♠ K1086
                 ♥ 53
                 ♦ AK109
                 ♣ 742
   ♠ QJ5                      ♠ 7432
   ♥ K76          N           ♥ 1092
   ♦ 83        W     E        ♦ 7642
   ♣ KQ1085       S           ♣ J3
                 ♠ A9
                 ♥ AQJ84
                 ♦ QJ5
                 ♣ A96
```

	South	North
	1 ♥	1 ♠
	2NT	3NT

Contract: 3NT by South. Lead ♣K.

Declarer has eight tricks on top and good prospects of making extras either from spades or, more likely, from hearts. However, West gets away to the best lead of the ♣K and East – correctly – unblocks with the jack enabling West to continue the suit in safety. Declarer wins the third round of clubs and before committing himself in the majors plays off his winning diamonds, throwing a small heart from his own hand.

Remember, declarer can't always see through the back of the cards.

West has to make two discards on the diamonds but really has only one spare card, a heart. If he throws a club all chance of defeating the contract will have gone, and since declarer is marked with the ♠A on the bidding and the K10 are in dummy a discard from the ♠QJ5 is most unattractive. That leaves the heart suit, and although it looks dangerous to unguard the king it is easily West's best shot. So his two discards should be the six and seven of hearts. After all, South doesn't know that the ♥K is now singleton so it is more than likely that he will pin his hopes on the finesse and West will make his king plus four clubs to defeat the contact.

One word of warning. Decide on your discards as soon as declarer starts to cash his diamonds (or before, if you like), then you will not have to go into a tell-tale trance when the fourth diamond is played.*

*It is true that South should play to better advantage by laying down the ♥A because, if the king doesn't drop, he won't mind losing a heart trick to East – the safe hand. However, that is his problem not West's.

Plan your discards early.

don't block the suit

Declarer soon learns that it can be absolutely fatal to block a suit but it is not quite so obvious for a defender looking at his own hand and dummy's. However, if defenders make a habit of returning the correct card – higher of the two remaining and the original fourth highest from a long suit – and also bear in mind the Rule of Eleven, they will seldom come to much harm.

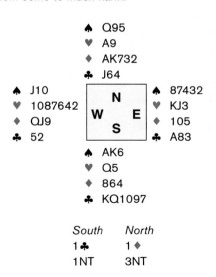

```
               ♠ Q95
               ♥ A9
               ♦ AK732
               ♣ J64
  ♠ J10          ┌─────────┐     ♠ 87432
  ♥ 1087642      │    N    │     ♥ KJ3
  ♦ QJ9          │ W     E │     ♦ 105
  ♣ 52           │    S    │     ♣ A83
                 └─────────┘
               ♠ AK6
               ♥ Q5
               ♦ 864
               ♣ KQ1097
```

South	North
1♣	1♦
1NT	3NT

Contract: 3NT by South. Lead ♥6.

West leads the ♥6 and Easts wins with the king. Now, suppose East is unwilling to jettison his ♥J under the ace, although it is usually correct to return the higher of two remaining cards, the suit is now blocked. Declarer will have to knock-out the ♣A, no doubt fearing the worst, but when East wins he can do no more than cash his ♥J. Thus the contract is made with an overtrick. But if East returns the ♥J at Trick 2 the suit is now freed and declarer will go two down. A big swing.

East has one more guideline, the Rule of Eleven. Six from eleven leaves five. So there are five cards better than the six between the other three hands. East can see four of them so he knows that South holds only one card to beat the six in which case it cannot cost to play the jack.

Consider unblocking a high card in partner's suit.

attitude signals

Signals play an important part in defense and fall into three main groups. Attitude signals (or Encouraging and Discouraging signals) are the most widely used.

When you follow suit with a high card and then a lower one – sometimes called Petering – you are encouraging your partner to continue. Conversely, if you follow with, say, the two and then the eight you are showing a lack of interest.

Play high-low to encourage.

Against Four Spades, West, your partner leads the ♣A. You, East, hold the ♣74 and would like to trump the third round. So you play the ♣7 on the ace and if, as expected, your partner continues with the king you complete the peter with the four. The play of the cards in this order – high-low – says 'I like it, carry on'. Obviously if you hold ♣742 you would have no reason to encourage your partner and therefore would play the two on his ace.

Sometimes you wish to encourage partner for reasons other than trumping the third round.

```
              962
    KQ74                J83
              A105
```

West, your partner, leads the king and since he no doubt has the queen as well (you play the ace from ace-king etc. and the king from king-queen etc.) you would like to give him the good news, so you follow with the eight. Had your original holding been three small (853) then you would have followed with your lowest card.

You can also indicate to your partner whether you like, or perhaps control, a suit by discarding a high card in that suit (the highest you can afford). This signal can help partner in two ways. First of all, if he is uncertain about his own discards he now knows which suit you are looking after. Secondly, if he obtains the lead he can play the suit in which you are strong.

So, Attitude Signals are a means of saying to partner, 'Yes, I like it', or 'No, I can't help'.

count signals

Experienced players sometimes help each other in defense by giving their count, especially in a critical suit. This is done by petering – playing high-low – with an even number and following upwards in natural order with an odd number.

Suppose the contract on the following hand is 3NT by South, and this is the club suit with no outside entries to dummy.

♣ KQJ108

♣ 742   ♣ A93

♣ 65

Declarer plays the ♣6 to dummy's king and obviously East will hold off on the first round, but when declarer continues with the ♣Q should he win or should he duck? In fact, everything hinges on the signal that West has given. In this case West would play the two to the first trick. This shows an odd number of cards so East would be correct to win the second round. However, it might be

Play high-low to show an even number of cards in that suit.

disastrous for him to do so if South held three clubs and West two. If this were the case West would start a peter with the seven (from **74**) and so help East to avert a disaster.

The full hand:

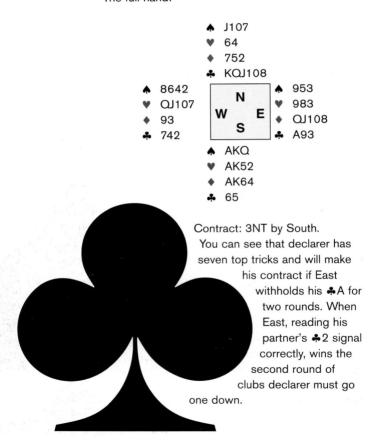

```
              ♠  J107
              ♥  64
              ♦  752
              ♣  KQJ108
  ♠  8642                    ♠  953
  ♥  QJ107      N            ♥  983
  ♦  93       W   E          ♦  QJ108
  ♣  742        S            ♣  A93
              ♠  AKQ
              ♥  AK52
              ♦  AK64
              ♣  65
```

Contract: 3NT by South.
You can see that declarer has seven top tricks and will make his contract if East withholds his ♣A for two rounds. When East, reading his partner's ♣2 signal correctly, wins the second round of clubs declarer must go one down.

suit preference signals

This signal is sometimes referred to as McKenney and, although it can be used in a number of different ways, I am going to concentrate on its most practical use which is concerned with obtaining ruffs.

Put yourself in the West position, defending Four Hearts.

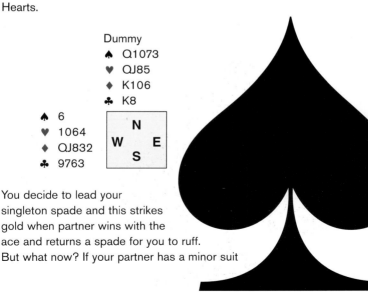

Dummy
- ♠ Q1073
- ♥ QJ85
- ♦ K106
- ♣ K8

- ♠ 6
- ♥ 1064
- ♦ QJ832
- ♣ 9763

```
      N
  W       E
      S
```

You decide to lead your singleton spade and this strikes gold when partner wins with the ace and returns a spade for you to ruff. But what now? If your partner has a minor suit ace you could put him in again for a second ruff and defeat the contract. But which suit should you choose, diamonds or clubs? The answers lies in the card that East plays back for you to ruff. If it is a big one, you play a diamond, if it is a small one, you play a club.

The McKenney signal works like this. You ignore the trump suit and the suit being led. That leaves two remaining suits, in this case diamonds and clubs. if partner wants the higher of these two suits − diamonds − he plays a high spade, and if he wants the lower − clubs − he plays a low spade. In fact, he returns the ♠2 so West, having ruffed, plays the nine or seven of clubs. East wins with the ace and gives his partner a second ruff to defeat the contract.

A high card calls for the higher ranking suit.

This is the full deal:

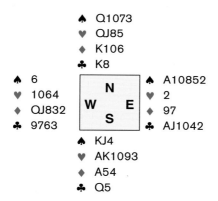

♠ Q1073
♥ QJ85
♦ K106
♣ K8

♠ 6
♥ 1064
♦ QJ832
♣ 9763

♠ A10852
♥ 2
♦ 97
♣ AJ1042

♠ KJ4
♥ AK1093
♦ A54
♣ Q5

Contract: 4 ♥ by South. Lead ♠6.

It should be remembered that all the signals you give to your partner are also available to declarer, so it is best to use them when you are reasonably sure that partner will be the main beneficiary, not declarer.

glossary

Balanced Hand	A hand in which the suits are evenly, or nearly evenly distributed. 4-3-3-3, 4-4-3-2 or 5-3-3-2 are the hand patterns in this category.
Blocking a Suit	Retaining a high card in the shorter holding of a suit which then prevents the suit being cashed.
Cashing	Cashing tricks means taking those that are there and available to be collected without having to resort to any special play.

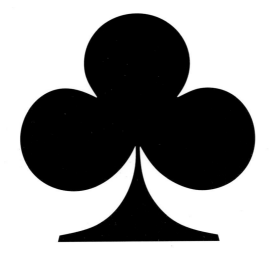

Contract

The final bid, which is followed by three passes, becomes the contract. Making the contract is winning the number of tricks promised by the bid.

Count

Giving partner the count is done by the order in which you play your cards. Following high/low usually shows an even number of cards while following upwards shows an odd number.

Declarer

Declarer is the player whose responsibility it is to fulfill the contract. He has become declarer because he bid the suit in which he is playing first.

Defenders	The defenders are the pair opposing declarer and his dummy.
Discarding	When you are unable to follow suit, you discard. That is to say you throw a card from another suit.
Distribution	How the cards are divided in a hand according to lengths and shortages – sometimes called shape.
Doubleton	Just two cards only in a suit.
Down	When a player goes down he has failed to fulfill his contract and consequently has to concede a penalty.
Drawing Trumps	Taking the opponents trumps away from them.
Ducking	Deliberately refusing to take a trick by playing a low card when a higher one is available. The idea is that the high card(s) may be used to greater advantage later in the play.

Dummy

Dummy is declarer's partner who takes no part in the play of the hand. The dummy hand is the hand which is exposed on the table.

Eliminate

To play out winners, and perhaps losers as well, from dummy's and declarer's hands so that the opposition when thrown on lead are unable to play the suit or suits concerned to advantage.

End-Play

Throwing a player on lead – usually towards the end of the game – so that, hopefully, he is forced to concede an extra trick.

Entries	High cards that enable a player to reach his partner's hand.
Establishing	Making a suit good, either by ruffing the losers or conceding a trick to achieve the same purpose.
Finessing	Playing towards split honors is the hope of capturing the missing honor(s). For example, lead small to AQ, AQ10, KJ, AJ10. But a finesse can also be taken at much lower levels e.g. lead small to 108 hoping to find the 9 well-placed.
Hold-up	Deliberately not taking a trick with a high card when one is available.
Major Suits	Spade and Hearts.

Minor Suits	Diamonds and Clubs.
Opener	The first player to bid.
Opening Lead	The original lead made by the defender on declarer's left.
Overcall	A bid made over an opponent's bid.
Pass	The same as No Bid.
Peter	A signal to partner by playing high/low, say the 8 followed by the 4.

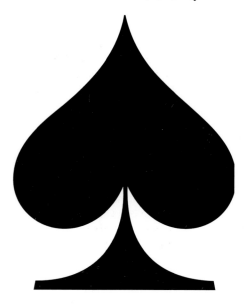

Post-Mortem | A term applied to the discussion of the hand at the conclusion of play.

Ruffing | Trumping when having none of the suit led.

Ruff and Sluff | Leading a suit in which dummy and declarer have none while they both still hold trumps. This enables declarer to ruff in one hand and discard a loser from the other.

Safe Lead | Playing a suit that will not give the opposition an extra trick.

Sequence | A run of three cards or more with no break in the consecutive order e.g. AKQ, KQJ, QJ10, 9876.

Shape	The way the cards are distributed in a hand.
Side Suit	A suit other than the trump suit.
Singleton	One card only in a suit.
Slam	Twelve winning tricks by declarer constitutes a Small Slam and all thirteen tricks a Grand Slam.
Tenace	Two cards in the same suit, one of which is higher than the missing card and one lower e.g. AQ, KJ, Q10, 108.
Trebleton	Three cards only in a suit.
Void	Having no cards in one of the suits.

Batsford Bridge Books

How to Play Bridge: Getting Started
Freddie North
£5.99   96 pp

How to Play Bridge: It's Your Bid
Tony Sowter
£5.99   96 pp

How to Play Bridge: Playing With Trumps
Sally Brock
£5.99   96 pp

How to Play Bridge: No Trump Play
Raymond Brock
£5.99   96 pp

How to Play Bridge: It's Your Lead
Brian Senior
£5.99   96 pp

Bridge: Basic Defence
Freddie North
£9.99   96 pp
*This basic volume covers simple signalling and
other basic themes.*

Bridge the Vital Principles
Freddie North
£8.99   128 pp
*One of the game's top teachers explores common
situations that confront any intermediate player.*

Cards at Play
Freddie North
£8.99   144 pp
Describes a wide range of the major technques available to declarer.

First Principles of Card Play
Paul Marston
£6.99   128 pp
Equally suitable for club players and social rubber-bridge players.

Learn Bridge in Five Days
Terence Reese
£6.99   112 pp
This quick introduction to the game covers all the essential aspects.

Step-by-Step Card Play in No Trumps
Robert Berthe and Norbert Lébely
£8.99   144 pp

Step-by-Step Card Play in Suits
Brian Senior
£8.99   144 pp

Step-by-Step Competitive Bidding
Tony Sowter
£8.99   144 pp

Step-by-Step Constructive Bidding
Tony Sowter
£8.99   144 pp

All books are availablefrom:
B T Batsford Ltd,
583 Fulham Road,
London SW6 5BY
Tel: +44 (171) 471 1100
Fax: +44 (171) 471 1101